LAZARUS

LAZARUS

A musical by **David Bowie**
and **Enda Walsh**

Inspired by *The Man Who Fell to Earth*
by Walter Tevis

THEATRE COMMUNICATIONS GROUP
NEW YORK
2017

Lazarus is published by Theatre Communications Group, Inc., 520 Eighth Avenue, 24th Floor, New York, NY 10018-4156

This volume is published in arrangement with Nick Hern Books Limited, The Glasshouse, 49a Goldhawk Road, London, W12 8QP.

This publication is made possible in part by the New York State Council on the Arts with the support of Governor Andrew Cuomo and the New York State Legislature.

TCG books are exclusively distributed to the book trade by Consortium Book Sales and Distribution.

A catalogue record for this book is available from the Library of Congress.

ISBN 978-1-55936-543-7 (paperback)

ISBN 978-1-55936-878-0 (ebook)

Cover design by Jacqueline Bodley

Cover image by iStockPhoto.com/abracada & RavenHD

Inside front cover photo by Jan Versweyveld (Michael C. Hall in *Lazarus*)

Inside back cover photo by Frank W. Ockenfels 3 (David Bowie)

First TCG Edition, March 2017

CONTENTS

THIS WAY OR NO WAY, YOU KNOW I'LL BE FREE

Enda Walsh

David Bowie had passed me a four-page document to read so we could begin our discussions on writing a new story with his songs, and based upon the character of Thomas Newton from the Walter Tevis novel *The Man Who Fell to Earth* – which David had famously played in the Nicolas Roeg film. In the room was the theatre and film producer Robert Fox and David's right hand, Coco Schwab. As I started to read those four pages, the room was very quiet.

Earlier, I had been feeling very calm and detached as I walked towards David's building with Robert – as we stood in the elevator, as that ridiculously wide office door opened, and Mr David Bowie was standing there. He hugged me and the first thing he said to me was, 'You've been in my head for three weeks.' We sat and we chatted about my work (he had read everything) and why I was writing the way I was – and what themes kept returning into my plays like a nasty itch. I spent that whole morning and now this first hour of our first meeting in a state of serene self-confidence.

It was only at the moment when he said, 'This is where I'd like to start,' when he pushed those four pages towards me, that I was hit with the realisation that I was sitting opposite this cultural icon – this man who had created so much and influenced so many. This bloody genius. David Fucking Bowie. I felt like a child – and at that point of silently 'reading' – a child who had once the ability to read words but had forgotten how to read. I scanned the first page and all I heard was interference – my own insecurities screaming at me.

I stopped reading, took a deep breath and read from the first line again.

David had written three new characters around Thomas Newton (the stranded alien, seemingly immortal and definitely stuck). There was a Girl who may or may not be real; a 'mass murderer' called Valentine; and a character of a woman who thought she might be Emma Lazarus (the American poet whose poem 'The New Colossus' is engraved on the base of the Statue of Liberty) – a woman in this case who would help and fall in love with this most travelled of immigrants: Thomas Newton.

At the centre of these four pages was a simple, powerful image: Thomas Newton would build a rocket from debris. His mind, having further deteriorated, would torture and tease him with the dream of escape; and in his imprisonment – in his room in this big tower – Newton would try one last time to leave.

So this is where we started.

We talked around the characters and the themes of the book. On isolation and madness and drug abuse and alcoholism and the torment of immortality. And there was a lot of talk about the beauty of unconditional love and goodness. We talked about characters finding themselves out of control – about the story sliding into a murky sadness and quick violence – about characters having drab conversations about television snacks – the everyday bending quickly and becoming Greek tragedy. The celestial and the shitty pavement.

For the first few meetings, Coco stayed silent and listened to us (until she couldn't listen to us any more maybe!), and then she asked, 'Yeah, but what happens?' It was a fair question and one

that we would return to – but we weren't there yet. We needed
to get a sense of the themes of it and its atmosphere and its
world. The narrative trajectory of a man wanting to leave Earth
and being helped by some and stopped by others – this was
there in David's four pages and would remain in our story, but
the events of the story would emerge later.

And then there were the songs.

David handed me a folder of lyrics and CDs he had put
together. 'Some of these you'll know.' It was a bloody funny
thing to say. We would hammer out the story together, but
initially he wanted me to choose the songs we would use.
I guess he had lived with some of them for years and there must
have been unshakable associations – maybe it would be easier
for me to listen to them coldly from a purely narrative
perspective.

His lyrics often arrive cut-up and opaque – so it was rarely
about listening to the words and sticking it into the story. It was
about the emotion, rhythm and atmosphere of those songs – and
having the characters riding that wave and accessing their souls,
where they could lyrically go to those strange places.

We talked about the form – the shape of the story arriving
broken and a little shattered. We talked about a person dying
and the moments before death and what might happen in their
mind and how that would be constructed onstage. We started
talking about escape, but we ended up talking about a person
trying to find rest. About dying in an easier way.

Newton would spend his last moments trying to stop a bullying
mind that kept him living. Physically it didn't matter to us
whether he was on Earth or in the stars at the very end. We
wanted Newton – in his terms – to feel at rest.

No matter how plays come out, you always end up talking
about yourself. David was certainly the most superb
shapeshifter – one of the greatest ever collaborators too –
someone who could walk his colleagues in directions they'd yet
seen. But for me he remained personal in his work and spoke
about where he was at that moment in really truthful terms.

Lazarus arrived at both of us with its own swagger and shape and emotion. It's a strange, difficult and sometimes sad dream Newton must live through – but in its conclusion, he wins his peace.

Lazarus was first performed at the New York Theatre Workshop (James C. Nicola, Artistic Director; Jeremy Blocker, Managing Director) by special arrangement with Robert Fox and Risky Folio, Inc., on 7 December 2015 (previews from 18 November). The cast was as follows:

NEWTON	Michael C. Hall
VALENTINE	Michael Esper
GIRL	Sophia Anne Caruso
ELLY	Cristin Milioti
TEENAGE GIRL 1	Krystina Alabado
TEENAGE GIRL 2	Krista Pioppi
TEENAGE GIRL 3	Brynn Williams
ZACH	Bobby Moreno
BEN	Nicholas Christopher
MICHAEL	Charlie Pollock
MAEMI	Lynn Craig

Composer/Writer	David Bowie
Writer	Enda Walsh
Director	Ivo van Hove
Scenic and Lighting Design	Jan Versweyveld
Costume Design	An D'Huys
Video Design	Tal Yarden
Sound Design	Brian Ronan
Musical Director	Henry Hey
Choreographer	Annie-B Parson
Dramaturg	Jan Peter Gerrits
Stage Manager	James Latus
Casting Director	Telsey + Company

Lazarus received its European premiere at the King's Cross Theatre, London, produced by Robert Fox and Jones/Tintoretto Entertainment, on 8 November 2016 (previews from 25 October). The cast was as follows:

NEWTON	Michael C. Hall
VALENTINE	Michael Esper
GIRL	Sophia Anne Caruso
ELLY	Amy Lennox
TEENAGE GIRL 1	Maimuna Memon
TEENAGE GIRL 2	Gabrielle Brooks
TEENAGE GIRL 3	Sydnie Christmas
ZACH	Richard Hansell
BEN	Jamie Muscato
MICHAEL	Tom Parsons
MAEMI	Julie Yammanee

Composer/Writer	David Bowie
Writer	Enda Walsh
Director	Ivo van Hove
Scenic and Lighting Design	Jan Versweyveld
Costume Design	An D'Huys
Video Design	Tal Yarden
Sound Design	Tony Gayle
Musical Supervisor and Orchestrations	Henry Hey
Choreographer	Annie-B Parson
Hair and Wig Design	Richard Mawbey
UK Casting Director	Jill Green Casting

LAZARUS

CHARACTERS

MICHAEL

NEWTON

ELLY

ZACH

JAPANESE WOMAN / MAEMI

TEENAGE GIRL 1

TEENAGE GIRL 2

TEENAGE GIRL 3

GIRL, *later* MARLEY

VALENTINE

BEN

LIST OF SONGS

'Lazarus' *Newton*

'It's No Game (Part 1)' *Japanese Woman, Newton, Teenage Girls*

'This is Not America' *Teenage Girls, Girl*

'The Man Who Sold the World' *Michael*

'No Plan' *Girl*

'Love is Lost' *Valentine, Teenage Girls*

'Changes' *Elly, Teenage Girls*

'Where Are We Now?' *Newton*

'Absolute Beginners' *Newton, Elly, Valentine, Teenage Girls, Girl*

'Dirty Boys' *Valentine*

'Killing a Little Time' *Newton*

'Life On Mars?' *Girl*

'All the Young Dudes' *Ben, Teenage Girls, Maemi*

'Always Crashing in the Same Car' *Elly*

'Valentine's Day' *Valentine*

'When I Met You' *Newton, Teenage Girl 1*

'Heroes' *Newton, Marley*

This text went to press before the end of rehearsals and so may differ slightly from the play as performed.

In the darkness a sudden cacophony of televisual sounds is heard.

It lights NEWTON – *he sits detached – staring into a screen – the television switching between channels – Ricky Nelson's 'Hello Mary Lou (Goodbye Heart)' skips/repeats in broken pieces.*

The sounds mix, distort and escalate – until suddenly they snap into silence.

MICHAEL. I'm sorry I haven't been around – it's been on my mind – but what with work and life and – you know. (*Slight pause.*) So I was looking through old photographs and it's weird – all these years I've known you – I find only the one photo of us from work together – this snap someone took.

Handing the photo to NEWTON –

You're the exact same – but I've got all this hair on me – the darkest, blackest hair – like it's been painted on.

ELLY *hands* NEWTON *his Lucky Charms.*

NEWTON (*to* ELLY). Thank you.

ELLY. You wanna bowl of something?

MICHAEL. Of cereal?

ELLY. Yeah.

MICHAEL. No, I'm good.

ELLY *turns away.*

So you okay? – you look all right – you don't look too bad – maybe a little scruffier. It's one of the many benefits of being retired, I suppose. So what do you do all day in here? Read all those books you always wanted to?

NEWTON. I watch television and drink gin.

4

MICHAEL. And that's it – you don't do anything else?

NEWTON. I walk around and try to locate the Twinkies.

MICHAEL. So a little bit of exercise too.

NEWTON. Yeah a little.

MICHAEL. But don't you miss the business at all?

NEWTON. No.

MICHAEL. Yeah you do.

NEWTON. No I don't. You wanna drink?

MICHAEL. It's 9.30, Mr Newton.

NEWTON. Is it?

MICHAEL. Yes, it is.

NEWTON. Oh.

MICHAEL. In the morning – 9.30 in the morning.

NEWTON. So late.

    NEWTON *pours himself a gin.*

MICHAEL. Anyway I'm sorry it's taken me forever – I feel
    bad. I could swing by next week – if you wanted it? I'd like
    to – you wouldn't mind me looking in?

NEWTON. I was sitting here in the middle of the night and the
    television went off and I saw something come out from the
    darkness. It's a scene I couldn't think about for years – and it
    came to me the way a lot of these things do – in these
    pictures. (*Slight pause.*) It was morning time and I was
    sitting at home with my wife and son and daughter – and
    nothing special happened – just small talk between us that I
    can't remember now – but I was there at home for a few
    moments with them. It was cruel in a way.

MICHAEL. You need to talk to someone – a doctor –

NEWTON. No.

MICHAEL. Don't you remember the person you were? – your life outside…

NEWTON. That was before.

MICHAEL. And it's gone? All of it?

NEWTON. Of course it's gone.

MICHAEL. But this isn't living for a man like you – eating Lucky Charms, living on gin and fucking Twinkies…

NEWTON. There's nothing of the past. It left. This is it now.

MICHAEL. Right. (*Slight pause.*) So you never see her?

NEWTON *doesn't answer.*

Did you hear me, Thomas? Do you ever see Mary-Lou?

A slight pause.

NEWTON. Only in my head.

The introduction to 'Lazarus' starts.

MICHAEL *embraces* NEWTON – *and leaves the apartment.*

LAZARUS

(*Newton.*) Look up here, I'm in heaven
I've got scars that can't be seen
I've got drama, can't be stolen
Everybody knows me now
Look up here, man, I'm in danger
I've got nothing left to lose

I'm so high it makes my brain whirl
I dropped my cellphone down below
Ain't that just like me
By the time I got to New York
I was living like a king
Then I used up all my money
I was looking for your ass

This way or no way
You know, I'll be free
Just like that bluebird
Ain't that just like me

And I'll be free
Just like that bluebird
Oh I'll be free
Ain't that just like me

ZACH. So what's he like?

ELLY. Sorta sad – sorta unknowable in the way that you
    imagine reclusive-rich-eccentric-men to be.

ZACH. Sounds amazing – is he good looking?

ELLY. Kind of freakishly young looking – had a shitload of
    work done, I guess.

ZACH. So you're attracted to him.

ELLY. Yeah my life is so starved of good-looking men – it would
    be impossible not to fall in love with him after two days.

ZACH. You slut! – so is he with anyone?

ELLY. Not now – he was once. He's lost – a little strange too.

ZACH. So it's just you. You and him. His maid.

ELLY. His assistant.

ZACH. His assistant, right. You assist him – got it.

ELLY. Asshole.

ZACH. I only wanna know what my wife is doing at work – I
    think that's fair.

ELLY. Don't talk to me like that! – Jesus Christ!

ZACH. Like what?

ELLY. 'My wife.'

ZACH. Well fuck it, Elly, you are my wife.

ELLY. Yeah but you referred to me as my wife while looking in my face. 'My wife.' 'This is my wife.'

ZACH. So will you stick with it?

ELLY. The job?

ZACH. Do you think being an assistant will fulfil you?

ELLY. I know you think my résumé's been written by squirrels – while your love of information technology has been handed down from Moses. Will it 'fulfil' me, Zach?!

ZACH. Maybe it will – I hope it does.

ELLY. And why do you hope that?

ZACH. Because I want my wife to be fulfilled – obviously not romantically fulfilled with Thomas fucking Newton.

ELLY. You know maybe I'm romantically fulfilled with you.

ZACH. Absolutely – I'm a very attractive man and you're a beautiful and compassionate wife.

ELLY. I'm a terrible wife – when was the last time we had sex? In what area of my life have I ever been successful?

ZACH. There are plenty of areas. Hundreds.

ELLY. Gimme one.

ZACH can't think of one.

I have to do something with my life. I used to have dreams a long time ago, d'you remember that? I used to have a sunny personality. Now I'm a shitty pool.

ZACH. Don't – come on.

A pause.

ELLY. I'm going to load the dishwasher and when I return I think we should try and have sexual intercourse.

ZACH. Sounds good.

A slight pause.

ELLY. I'll probably need a sandwich first.

ZACH. Yeah me too.

The introduction to 'It's No Game (Part 1)' blasts.

A JAPANESE WOMAN *is heard amplified –*

IT'S NO GAME (PART 1)

(*Japanese Woman.*) Shirneto yak age ga –
– kakumei o miteiru
Mo tengokuno giu no kaidan wa nai

NEWTON *responds –*

(*Newton.*) Silhouettes and shadows watch the revolution
No more – free steps to heaven
It's no
(*Newton and Teenage Girls.*) game
(*Teenage Girls.*) Oh – ooo

NEWTON*'s laughing – his day's hard drinking is kicking in.*

The JAPANESE WOMAN *responds from the television –*

(*Japanese Woman.*) Ore genjitsu kara shime dasare
Nani ga okkote iru ka wakara nai
Doko ni kyokun wa aruka

Suddenly the JAPANESE WOMAN *sweeps into the apartment wearing a traditional kimono – it's like they're old friends.*

NEWTON. Ohayo gozaimasu!

(*Newton.*) Hitobito wa yabi o orareteiru
Konna dokusaisha ni igashime rareru nowa kanashi

NEWTON *watches her perform a Japanese tea ceremony.*

I am barred from the event
I really don't understand the situation
(*Newton and Teenage Girls.*) But it's no game

The TEENAGE GIRLS, *sing from their world –*

Documentaries on refugees
Couples 'gainst the target
You throw the rock against the road
And it breaks into pieces
Draw the blinds on yesterday
And it's all so much scarier
Put a bullet in my brain
And it makes all the papers

(*Japanese Woman*.) Nammino kiroku eiga
Hioteki o se ni shita koibi to tach
Michi ni ishi o nage reba
Konago na mi kudake
Kino mi hutao sureba
Kyohu wa masu
Ore no atama ni tama o buchi kome ba
Shimbun wa kaki tateru

(*Newton*.) So where's the moral when people have their
    fingers broken
To be insulted by these fascists – it's so degrading
And it's no game.
Shut up! Shut up!

*He stumbles, falls over and smashes the side of his head on
the ground.*

The music screeches to a stop. Silence.

The music to 'This is Not America' begins –

NEWTON. In this sleep of death – what dreams may come…

A light comes up on the face of a young teenage GIRL.

THIS IS NOT AMERICA

(*Teenage Girls*.) This is not America
Sha-la-la-la-la

(*Girl*.) A little piece of you
The little piece in me
Will die

(*Teenage Girls*.) This is not the miracle
(*Girl*.) For this is not America

Blossom fails to bloom
This season
Promise not to stare
Too long
For this is not the miracle

NEWTON *looks at this new vision developing.*

There was a time
A storm that blew so pure
This could be the biggest sky
I could have
The faintest idea.
(*Teenage Girls*.) For this is not America
(*Girl*.) Sha-la-la-la-la
(*Teenage Girls*.) This is not America
(*Girl*.) No
(*Teenage Girls*.) This is not
Sha la-la-la-la

(*Girl*.) Snowman melting
From the inside
Falcon spirals
To the ground
(*Teenage Girls*.) This could be the biggest sky
(*Girl*.) So bloody red
Tomorrow's clouds

A little piece of you
The little piece in me
Will die

(*Teenage Girls*.) This could be the miracle
(*Girl*.) For this is not America

There was a time
A wind that blew so young
For this could be the biggest sky
I could have the faintest idea
(*Teenage Girls*.) For this is not America
(*Girl*.) Sha-la-la-la-la
(*Teenage Girls*.) This is not America
(*Girl*.) No
(*Girl and Teenage Girls*.) Sha-la-la-la-la

GIRL. Do you need any help?

NEWTON. Some help – yes.

GIRL. D'you know what happened?

NEWTON. Yeah the floor hit me.

GIRL. You should replace it with another floor.

NEWTON. Good thinking – I'll do that. You wanna drink?

GIRL. No thanks.

NEWTON. A teetotaller, right. So what's your name?

GIRL. I don't know.

NEWTON. You don't have a name?

GIRL. Well I must have a name but I can't remember it just
now.

NEWTON. You seem incredibly calm about that.

GIRL. Yeah I know – it's odd. You know up close you look
really sick? You're not dying are you?

NEWTON. A little bit every day. I'm a dying man who can't die
actually.

GIRL. That's a joke, right?

NEWTON. Not being able to die is a joke. A fucking terrible joke. Apologies for the f-word.

GIRL. You know, your apartment smells a little bit – maybe if you got a scented candle or sprayed a little Glade…

NEWTON. Sorry but what exactly are you doing here?

GIRL. Well right now I'm talking to you.

NEWTON. No you think you're talking to me.

GIRL. What do you mean?

NEWTON. You're not real.

GIRL. I feel real.

NEWTON. Well you're not. My brain's just making you up – which will come as a terrible disappointment – but you're just another dream, a delusion, a chemical belch in my head! Moments ago Mary-Lou was dancing inside that television… which is impossible.

The music to 'The Man Who Sold the World' begins –

You hear that!?

GIRL. What?

NEWTON. Music.

MICHAEL *is seen –*

THE MAN WHO SOLD THE WORLD

(*Michael.*) We passed upon the stair
We spoke of was and when
Although I was not there
He said I was his friend

Which came as some surprise
I spoke into his eyes
He must have died alone
A long long time ago.

Oh no, not me
I never lost control
You're face to face
With the Man Who Sold the World.

I laughed and shook his hand
And made my way back home
I searched for form and land
For years and years I roamed
I gazed a gazely stare
At all the millions here
We must have died alone
A long long time ago

Who knows? Not me
We never lost control
You're face to face
With the Man Who Sold the World.

NEWTON *sees* ELLY – *her back to him.*

NEWTON. Elly?

The light opens and NEWTON *sees that she's looking in at* ZACH *in their apartment.*

Elly – can you hear me?

ELLY *doesn't want to go in to* ZACH. *She turns away fast.*

NEWTON *follows her and collapses into his bed.*

(*Michael.*) Who knows? Not me
We never lost control
You're face to face
With the Man Who Sold the World.

Who knows? Not me
We never lost control
You're face to face
With the Man Who Sold the World.

The GIRL *is with three* TEENAGE GIRLS, *looking down at* NEWTON *in the bed*.

TG3. So when d'ya get here?

GIRL. I just turned up – before that I don't remember a thing.

TG1. So have you talked to him?

GIRL. Yeah a little – who is he?

TG3. You already know.

TG2. You know everything about him.

GIRL. I do?

TG1. You'll see.

GIRL. So what do we do exactly?

TG1. It's a lot of showin' up and listenin'.

TG2. They're all a bit messed up and tortured and stuff – but you figure things out for them and give them hope. Then you get to leave once the work is finished.

GIRL. He's a bit strange – you don't think I can work with someone else?

TG1. No.

VALENTINE *is in* MICHAEL*'s apartment –*

VALENTINE. Hi.

MICHAEL. What the fuck?!

VALENTINE. I was going to wait outside but your neighbour, Mrs Weissler – she suffers with insomnia – well she was out of her apartment and she invited me into hers – which was really nice.

MICHAEL. Stop talking.

VALENTINE. We had a good conversation about insomnia – 'cause I too don't sleep too well. It depresses her a little – but I prefer to be awake. Anyway, I pretended I was your brother and she gave me your spare key.

MICHAEL. If you don't leave I'll call the police.

VALENTINE. That's no way to treat a friend…

MICHAEL. You're not my friend – (*About his phone.*) The fucking shit…

VALENTINE. The battery's dead. You've gotta turn off Bluetooth…

MICHAEL. Look if you want money – I can write you a cheque.

VALENTINE. My God this is so unlike you! When we were young we were inseparable. People presumed that we were brothers, right? And I stood by you when you told your family that you were a gay man. D'you remember all that?!

MICHAEL. What are you saying…?!

VALENTINE. All those people we had grown up with in Tinto Falls just turned on you. But I was there – despite feeling uncomfortable with your life choice…

MICHAEL. This is a stupid mistake – I'm not the person you think I am…

VALENTINE. Yes you are.

MICHAEL. I'm not – for one thing – I'm fucking straight! Now get the fuck out of my apartment!

VALENTINE. I don't remember ever being rude to you, Mike. I never told you to f-off – I didn't call you names or make a judgement about you – and now it's like you're trying to pull yourself out of this situation – like you've already decided that I'm not a good person – while actually, Mike, I'm not altogether a bad person, you know!?

MICHAEL. Jesus.

The music to 'No Plan' begins.

A slight pause.

VALENTINE. God I'm sorry – I'll leave in a few minutes – I just need to gather my thoughts – this is completely out of character and… crazy of me. Apologies.

MICHAEL. It's all right. Take a moment and then just – go.

A slight pause.

VALENTINE. Can I sit down for a bit?

MICHAEL *watches him.*

I made the mistake of not eating today – or at least not eating much. I've got to watch my blood sugar – I'm such a doofus about that stuff.

A slight pause.

This is a lovely apartment by the way.

The light fades off them and up on NEWTON, *seated facing the* GIRL.

NO PLAN

    (*Girl.*) Here – there's no music here, I'm lost
In streams of sound
Here – am I nowhere now,
no plan
Where – ever I may go, just where
Just there I am

NEWTON *gets up and pours himself another large drink.*

    All of the things
That are my life, my desire, my beliefs, my moods
Here is my place, without a plan

    Here, 2nd Avenue
Just out of view
Here – is no traffic here, no plan

    All the things that are my life, my moods
My beliefs, my desires, me alone, nothing to regret
This is no place, but here I am,
This is not quite yet.

The music continues as the scene plays out –

GIRL. You asked me earlier what I was doing here.

NEWTON. I did.

GIRL. Well I'm supposed to help you in some way.

NEWTON. You could help me find another Twinkie.

GIRL. I think it's supposed to be help in the caring sense of the word, Mr Newton.

NEWTON. Like a very small nurse?

GIRL. Yeah. Maybe. I don't know.

A slight pause.

NEWTON. So you know my name?

GIRL. Yeah, you're Thomas Jerome Newton.

NEWTON. And what else do you know about me?

GIRL. That you're not from our world – which is a little weird – but true, right? Only a few people know that.

A light comes up on ELLY.

There's a tissue-wrapped garment near the bed – ELLY *opens it and lifts out a blouse.*

You were sent here from another planet and you never got back home to your family. You got real rich – started a bunch of companies. You tried to leave once before and these people did experiments on you and they hurt you really bad – turned you crazy – and you wouldn't prove what you were to them – and they stopped you leaving. And you were in love with this woman called Mary-Lou. But she left years ago – and you're still stuck here drinking gin and not being able to die or leave.

A slight pause.

That's why your head's sick. You're heartbroken over all of that stuff.

A slight pause.

I know your whole story and nothing of mine.

The music to 'No Plan' ends.

NEWTON (*to* ELLY). What are you doing?

ELLY. I'm sorry.

NEWTON. You've got clothes of your own – I've seen you wearing them – and you're being paid...

ELLY. This isn't your blouse, right? If it is, that's fine – if you wanna do dress-up in the safety of your own apartment...

NEWTON. It's not mine.

ELLY. Right. So why do you keep it? Just as a reminder of someone?

NEWTON. I don't need her things to remind me of her.

ELLY. Is she dead? You don't have to answer that.

NEWTON. I don't know.

ELLY. She just left you?

NEWTON. A long time ago.

ELLY. Did she love you?

NEWTON. Yes.

ELLY. Did you love her?

NEWTON. So many questions in such a small amount of time.

ELLY. I spent a summer doing market research for Macy's – I can ask thirty questions in under a minute.

NEWTON. Wow.

ELLY. It's the only thing I have a talent for. So did you love her?

NEWTON. Yes. (*Slight pause.*) Very much.

A slight pause.

ELLY. I think it's only fair that you get to ask me a question.

NEWTON. Don't you have someone to go home to?

ELLY. Yeah. I guess I have a husband.

NEWTON. Right. Then you should go.

A slight pause.

ELLY. What's it like to feel that much love for someone and to be loved back?

The introduction to 'Love is Lost' is heard.

ELLY *leaves the apartment.*

MICHAEL *is slumped opposite* VALENTINE – *dead.*

VALENTINE *puts* MICHAEL*'s jacket on.*

There's a small bit of blood on his hand. He wipes it off on his trousers.

He then takes the photograph that MICHAEL *had shown to* NEWTON *out of the jacket pocket.*

He sings –

LOVE IS LOST

(*Valentine.*) It's the darkest hour, you're twenty-two
The voice of youth, the hour of dread

Images from inside a packed bar appear on the walls.

NEWTON *walks slowly over to* MICHAEL – *and looks down at his dead body.*

MICHAEL *suddenly gets up – his shirt bloody – and leaves the apartment.*

VALENTINE *gets a drink and looks about the bar.*

The darkest hour and your voice is new
Love is lost, lost is love

Love everywhere is blossoming – images of people kissing – appear.

ELLY *and* ZACH *are locked in a piece of choreography detailing their shitty love life.*

NEWTON *sees this too – his hallucination – darkening for him.*

> Your country's new, your friends are new
> Your house and even your eyes are new
> Your maid is new and your accent too
> But your fear is as old as the world

VALENTINE *drinks.*

ELLY *and* ZACH *continue their charade.*

A light comes up on a beautiful couple.

Unseen – VALENTINE *moves closer to them – they are* MAEMI (*the same actress who played the* JAPANESE WOMAN) *and* BEN.

> (*Valentine and Teenage Girls.*) Say goodbye to the thrills
>   of life
> Where love was good, no love was bad
> Wave goodbye to the life without pain
> (*Valentine.*) Say hello (*Teenage Girls.*) ooo
> You're a beautiful girl
>
> Love is lost
> Oh, love is lost ooo
> Oh, love is lost ooo
> Oh, love is lost ooo

BEN *and* MAEMI *leave.*

VALENTINE *shouldn't follow them/doesn't want to follow them – but does.*

TEENAGE GIRL 1 *watches* VALENTINE.

ELLY *faces the wall and slowly draws a little red circle on it with her lipstick.*

> (*Valentine.*) Say hello to the lunatic men
> (*Teenage Girls.*) Say hello, hello

(*Valentine*.) Tell them your secrets
They're like the grave
(*Teenage Girls*.) Tell them all you know
(*Valentine*.) Oh, what have I done? Oh, what have I done?
(*Teenage Girls*.) They are like a grave
(*Valentine and Teenage Girls*.) Love is lost, lost is love

VALENTINE *remains standing still* – TEENAGE GIRL 1,
unseen, watches him.

(*Valentine*.) You know so much it's making you cry
(*Teenage Girls*.) You know, you know
(*Valentine*.) You refuse to talk but you think like mad
(*Teenage Girls*.) You know, you know

(*Valentine*.) You've cut out your soul and the face of
    thought
(*Teenage Girls*.) You know, you know, you know

ELLY *steps back from the wall slightly. She's holding a glass
in her hand.*

(*Valentine and Teenage Girls*.) Oh, what have you done?
    Oh, what have you done?

ELLY *smashes the glass into the wall.*

The music cuts and slides into the introduction to 'Changes'.

ELLY *stares down at the broken glass – she should clean up
the pieces – but she won't.*

*She picks little shards of glass out of her hand – as she
sings –*

CHANGES

(*Elly*.) I still don't know what I was waiting for
And my time was running wild
A million dead-end streets
And every time I thought I'd got it made

It seemed the taste was not so sweet
So I turned myself to face me
But I've never caught a glimpse
Of how the others must see the faker
I'm much too fast to take that test

She turns as a light comes up on ZACH, *sitting down, eating a bowl of cereal.*

(*Teenage Girls.*) Ch-ch-ch-ch-Changes

NEWTON *watches as a light comes up on the* TEENAGE
GIRLS –

(*Elly.*) Turn and face the strange.
(*Teenage Girls.*) Ch-ch-Changes
(*Elly.*) Don't want to be a richer one
(*Teenage Girls.*) Ch-ch-ch-ch-Changes
(*Elly.*) Turn and face the strange.

ELLY *goes and sits beside* ZACH *as he eats his cereal and reads from his phone.*

(*Teenage Girls.*) Ch-ch-Changes
(*Elly.*) Just gonna have to be a different one
Time may change me
But I can't trace time

There's a pressure on her – like she's trying to act polite and be the good wife.

I watch the ripples change their size
But never leave the stream
Of warm impermanence and
So the days float through my eyes

Ignored by ZACH *and she's behind him now – she brushes his hair gently with her hand – a surprising show of affection.*

But still the days seem the same
And these children that you spit on
As they try to change their worlds
Are immune to your consultations

They're quite aware of what they're going through
(*Teenage Girls.*) Ch-ch-ch-ch-Changes

Suddenly she pulls at his hair – ZACH's up fast – that fucking hurt.

He quickly goes to get his jacket to leave.

(*Elly.*) Turn and face the strange.

She stares at him – getting his work-shit together.

(*Teenage Girls.*) Ch-ch-Changes
(*Elly.*) Don't tell them to grow up and out of it
(*Teenage Girls.*) Ch-ch-ch-ch-Changes
(*Elly.*) Turn and face the strange.
(*Teenage Girls.*) Ch-ch-Changes
(*Elly.*) Where's your shame
You've left us up to our necks in it

ZACH *glances back at her – he should really kiss her goodbye – but neither of them can be bothered.*

Time may change me
But you can't trace time

ZACH *leaves – and left alone,* ELLY *dances with herself. Badly.*

NEWTON *is close to her now but she doesn't see him.*

Strange fascination, fascinating me
Changes are taking the pace
I'm going through
(*Teenage Girls.*) Ch-ch-ch-ch-Changes
(*Elly.*) Turn and face the strange.

There's another tissue-wrapped parcel – ELLY *opens it and takes out another blouse.*

(*Teenage Girls.*) Ch-ch-Changes
(*Elly.*) Oh, look out you rock'n'rollers
(*Teenage Girls.*) Ch-ch-ch-ch-Changes
(*Elly.*) Turn and face the strange.

She puts on the blouse.

> (*Teenage Girls.*) Ch-ch-Changes
> (*Elly.*) Pretty soon now you're gonna get older
> Time may change me
> But I can't trace time

NEWTON *looks up and the* GIRL *is walking over to him fast.*

> I said that time may change me
> But I can't trace time

The song ends –

GIRL. So I just figured out why I'm here.

NEWTON. I don't want to talk right now…

GIRL. You don't have to talk – you wanna hear my plan?

NEWTON. No.

GIRL. I'm here to get you out of this apartment – get you home to your own planet – I think we should build a rocket…

NEWTON (*his head hurts*). Fuck…

GIRL. You think it's a good idea?

NEWTON. A rocket out of what?

GIRL. Stuff.

NEWTON. So this isn't a rocket that will propel me through space?

GIRL. I haven't worked out the details just yet –

NEWTON. I've tried rocket-building before, you know that – with actual engineering…

GIRL. Yeah I know all about that.

> ELLY *is seen looking at him.*

NEWTON. Right – you know everything about me and nothing about you!

GIRL. You're stuck here heartbroken over Mary-Lou – I know that much! You forget about her and you can start making something else.

NEWTON. Like a rocket in my apartment?

GIRL. When you're stuck between two worlds – it's only right that you try something incredible…

NEWTON (*snaps*). Or something fucking insane! I need to sleep – just leave!

GIRL. You don't think I want to leave!? – I've no idea who I am or how I got here – but you're all I've got!

NEWTON. You're not a real girl – you're not here – you're inside here!! (*Hitting his head.*)

ELLY. What are you doing?

NEWTON *and the* GIRL *turn and see* ELLY.

What girl – who are you talking to?

NEWTON. She's nobody – nothing.

GIRL. I'll be back with reinforcements.

ELLY. I need to stay the night – I can't explain it.

NEWTON *watches the* GIRL *leave the apartment.*

I don't want to go home – I'll keep out of your way. Is that all right?

A slight pause.

What's wrong?

NEWTON. I'm frightened.

A slight pause.

ELLY. Why?

NEWTON. When you're not here I'm seeing you still. Others too… this man. If I haven't already – I think I'm about to break further.

ELLY. What can I do to help?

NEWTON. Nothing, it's too late. (*Slight pause.*) Stay if you like.

A pause.

ELLY. Thank you.

ELLY *leaves the light.*

A long pause as NEWTON *just stands alone.*

He cries momentarily – wipes his eyes – walks over and pours himself another drink.

He fills the glass to the brim and drinks it back.

He finds a record player on the ground – and turns it on.

He lowers the needle onto the record.

The opening strains to 'Where Are We Now?' begin to play.

WHERE ARE WE NOW?

(*Newton.*) Had to get the train
From Potsdamer Platz
You never knew that
That I could do that
Just walking the dead

Faint images appear on the walls around NEWTON *– of a repeated image of Mary-Lou slowly turning and looking towards him.*

Sitting in the Dschungel
On Nürnberger Strasse
A man lost in time
Near KaDeWe
Just walking the dead

Where are we now?
Where are we now?
The moment you know
You know you know

Twenty thousand people
Cross Bösebrücke
Fingers are crossed
Just in case
Where are we now?
Where are we now?
The moment you know
You know you know

As long as there's sun
As long as there's sun
As long as there's rain
As long as there's rain

As long as there's fire
As long as there's fire
As long as there's me
As long as there's you

A light comes up on VALENTINE *with* BEN – *as* BEN
studies the torn photograph –

BEN. Remember when he sold all his companies? Incredible.
He used to be the biggest name – everything he touched
turned gold – now he's nothing – like he never existed.

VALENTINE. Amazing, really.

BEN. It's old, hah? You just found it? And torn up like this –
strange.

VALENTINE. You and your girlfriend – you're very good
looking by the way.

BEN. Thank you.

VALENTINE. Have you been together long?

BEN. About a year. Getting married in a week actually.

VALENTINE. Oh congratulations! That's exciting.

BEN. Yeah.

> MAEMI *enters the light –*

> Hey, sweetie – just talking to this gentleman…

MAEMI. Hi there.

VALENTINE. Hey.

BEN. This is Maemi – I'm Ben by the way.

VALENTINE. Valentine. Nice to meet you.

MAEMI. What a nice name.

VALENTINE. I was just saying that you're a very striking couple, Maemi – very beautiful –

MAEMI. Oh.

VALENTINE. – and congratulations on your forthcoming nuptials.

MAEMI. Well thank you very much – it's something Ben likes to share with everyone.

VALENTINE. Saint Valentine is actually the patron saint of affianced couples so…

BEN. Oh really.

VALENTINE. So how did you guys meet?

> *A slight pause.*

BEN. You really want to hear about it?

VALENTINE. If you don't mind.

MAEMI. He's kidding!

VALENTINE. No no honestly!

BEN. Really?

VALENTINE. I'm a hopeless romantic – I just go doolally over all of that stuff.

BEN. Me too – completely.

MAEMI (*to* BEN). Tell him the story. He loves telling it anyway so…

BEN. Don't say it like that!

MAEMI. It's true! It's sweet – and a little weird – but tell it!

A slight pause.

BEN. Well I was in a cab – and we stopped at the lights – and Maemi was in a cab beside mine and we looked at one another through the windows.

And there was this big connection between us.…

VALENTINE. Right.

BEN. So the lights went green and my cab went straight on – while Maemi's turned the corner.

VALENTINE. Oh God no.

BEN. You could imagine, right? – I was destroyed!

The lights slowly close down on VALENTINE *and* TEENAGE GIRL 1 *as the sound of a fire alarm is faded up from quiet.*

For the rest of the journey I was sort of aching with what felt like a love lost. I was going to Brooklyn – to my colleague's house – a house I never visited before…

The alarm screaming now.

Lights up on NEWTON – *he's watching* ZACH *reaching upwards at a fire alarm roaring down on him – he feebly pokes at it to turn it off –*

ZACH. Fuckidy fuck – fuck off!

It turns off.

ELLY *is standing in the light in her jeans and T-shirt, holding a towel. She's just dyed her hair blue.*

(Seeing her.) Jesus Christ!

ELLY. What?

ZACH. What do you mean – 'What?' Your hair! When did you decide – what the fuck...

ELLY. So what?

ZACH. Is it something you've been thinking about?

ELLY. No.

ZACH. Was it an accident?

ELLY. Don't you like it? I don't care if you do or don't – it's not about you. It feels good.

ZACH. It looks terrible.

ELLY. Fuck you.

ZACH. You look like a lady Smurf.

ELLY. No I don't.

ZACH. A Smurfette! You look like a friggin' Smurfette!

ELLY. Smurfs have blue skin, you stupid asshole!

She dresses in a silk dress she took from NEWTON'*s apartment.*

ZACH. Are you trying to upset me?

ELLY. You don't think it's possible for me to act out something without ever thinking of your opinion...?

ZACH. You didn't think about anything – you've got blue fucking hair!!

ELLY. I know – I read the bottle!

ZACH. In the Smurf Village?

ELLY. I'm late.

ZACH. Is this about Newton?

ELLY. You'd love it if it was.

ZACH. Well is it?

ELLY. It's all you ever talk about – every other conversation is about whether I'm attracted to him or whether I'm fucking him…

ZACH. Are you fucking him? – you're spending a lot of time in his house.

ELLY. I work there!

ZACH. You stay over!

ELLY. No I don't…

ZACH. You stayed over last night.

ELLY. I did not!

ZACH. You can't remember that?

ELLY. You're a liar…

ZACH. Fuck it – are you looking after yourself?

ELLY. Shut up!

ZACH. You're not taking your pills? You want me to talk to your doctor – 'cause this shit isn't normal behaviour…!

ZACH is lost in the light.

NEWTON stands watching ELLY standing alone.

She holds her head – squeezing it slowly.

Suddenly the GIRL – dressed in a blue wig and silk dress – enters and walks towards NEWTON –

GIRL. Don't be scared – it's only a wig and a costume!

TEENAGE GIRL 2 and 3 enter from the other direction fast.

We're going to do a play based on your past.

TG2. It's autobiographical.

TEENAGE GIRL 3 *is dressed as* NEWTON.

TG3. I've only had a day's rehearsal – so don't go too harsh on my impersonation of you.

Suddenly ELLY *appears –*

ELLY. I'm sorry I'm so late. I'm late – you didn't know – it doesn't matter.

She can't see the TEENAGE GIRLS.

Do you want me to fix you a sandwich?

NEWTON. No.

TG2. Let's get started!

GIRL. It's your last conversation with Mary-Lou.

NEWTON. And why are you doing this?

GIRL. It's your therapy.

NEWTON. Right. Good.

TG2. Lights and sound, go!

Ricky Nelson singing 'Hello Mary Lou (Goodbye Heart)' is heard playing quietly.

GIRL (*a very bad Kentucky accent*). You won't ever get back home – you know that, Tommy. You got everything here in New York. You got me. This is your home now.

ELLY *just watches him.*

Why would you tell me you don't belong here – when I know you don't really think that…?

NEWTON (*to* ELLY). Why have you done that?

A slight pause in the performance.

ELLY. What do you mean…?

NEWTON. To your hair – why have you done that to yourself?

ELLY. I don't know why.

TG2 (*to the* GIRL). Next line, come on!

The scene resumes –

GIRL (*as Mary-Lou*). I know you have your family – but by the time you travel back home – even if you could – they'll probably be dead, Tommy.

TG3 (*as* NEWTON). Don't say that, Mary-Lou. That's a terrible thing to say.

ELLY *gets herself a large drink.*

GIRL. Well if you still want to leave – then you have to prove what you are to those people – they think you're just crazy. But you can leave if you show 'em that you're not one of us…

TG3. I've proved enough to them – they just hurt me and ehhh… (*Calls.*) Shit! What's the line?

NEWTON. I've gone as far as I can.

The GIRL *turns and looks at him – and still playing Mary-Lou –*

GIRL. Then you're going nowhere – and you'll be stuck in this apartment with me and I'll always know that you didn't wanna stay. Not with me you don't – not for me, Tommy.

ELLY *stands looking at him.*

You can't be in love with me any more – that's what you're telling me?

A slight pause.

Why are you making me go when I know that you still love me?

NEWTON. Because I have to.

A slight pause.

GIRL. You're going to rot like a fucking animal up here, you know that!? Just an animal – a stupid creature!

The GIRL *holds her face in her hands and pretends to cry.*

TEENAGE GIRL 2 *takes the record off.*

The play is over.

ELLY (*to* NEWTON). Why don't you tell me what's going on?

NEWTON. Because I can't.

ELLY. Tommy, please – I'm right here – there's nobody else...

NEWTON. I don't want you to call me that...!

ELLY. But that's what she called you, right...?

NEWTON. Stop it – don't!

A slight pause.

Please, Elly, I'm sorry – I can't explain...

A slight pause.

ELLY *leaves the light.*

The GIRL *takes off her blue wig.*

TG2. Right we're done.

A pause.

NEWTON. Tell me something I've told to no one.

GIRL. Like what?

NEWTON. A good memory I have.

A pause.

GIRL. You had a daughter my age. Your wife and son would
stay at home and you and your daughter use t'walk together
– you walked to this hill near your house – and reaching the
top of the hill you'd sit in the same place and watch the sky
filling with stars. You'd make up stories about travelling
through space and when you paused a little – your daughter
would say – 'Speak some more – and we'll travel on.'

A slight pause.

NEWTON. Thank you.

A pause.

GIRL. You knew that you'd end up like this. That's why you let Mary-Lou go. (*Slight pause.*) You don't have to stay here any longer, Mr Newton.

The GIRL *leaves.*

NEWTON *is left alone.*

He looks empty, finished.

After some moments –

ABSOLUTE BEGINNERS

(*Newton.*) I've nothing much to offer
There's nothing much to take

The music to 'Absolute Beginners' is heard –

I'm an absolute beginner
But I'm absolutely sane
(*Newton and Elly.*) As long as we're together
The rest can go to hell
I absolutely love you
But we're absolute beginners
With eyes completely open
But nervous all the same

VALENTINE *appears in a light, looking down at the photograph of* NEWTON.

(*Newton.*) If my love song
Could fly over mountains
Could laugh at the ocean
Just like the films

TEENAGE GIRL 1 *is seen walking towards him –*

(*Valentine and TG1.*) There's no reason
To feel all the hard times

To lay down the hard lines
It's absolutely true

TEENAGE GIRL 2 *and* 3 *sing the backing vocals* (*the 'Ba-ba-ba-oooos'*).

ELLY *staggers about drinking a glass of something –*

> (*Elly.*) Nothing much could happen
> Nothing I can't shake

She stands in the light of the television and sings for NEWTON *– and maybe she'll find some love here –*

> Oh I'm an absolute beginner
> With nothing much at stake
> As long as you're still smiling
> There's nothing more I need
> I absolutely love you
> But I'm an absolute beginner
> If my love is your love
> We're certain to succeed

He turns away from her and looks towards the GIRL.

> (*Newton/Girl/Valentine/Elly/Teenage Girls.*) If our love
>   song
> Could fly over mountains

The GIRL *turns and looks at* NEWTON –

> Could sail over heartache
> Just like the films

ELLY *is devastated by* NEWTON*'s rejection of her.*

TEENAGE GIRL 1 *stands with* VALENTINE, *looking at* ELLY. *She whispers in his ear, turns and leaves.*

> If there's reason
> To feel all the hard times
> To lay down the hard lines
> It's absolutely true

The music swirls triumphantly.

But NEWTON *– fragile still –*

NEWTON. If I don't go on – you'll have to help me.

A slight pause.

GIRL. So what is it you want?

Above them is turning blue.

NEWTON. To be back in the stars.

A slight pause.

GIRL. Then that's where we'll go.

The music surges.

In a light and ELLY *comes face to face with* VALENTINE.

He hands her the photograph of NEWTON.

The music abruptly cuts –

VALENTINE. I was walking past the building and something
   inside me told me to stop – and it felt like someone needed
   my help – so I step into the lobby and I see you coming out
   of the elevator and I see that you're crying, right? So do you
   love someone – you don't have to answer that – but is that
   why you were crying? – I think it might have been – you and
   Mr Newton – it's about you two being in love?

ELLY. I've only ever been raggedy with my life. Out of
   nowhere I get this job – and it gives me some reason to get
   up in the morning – but the more I stay in his apartment – the
   less I remember of the old me. And only one week passes but
   it feels like years – and I'm standing there with no
   personality of my own, with no idea of what I want to be.
   And I can feel Mary-Lou walk over and claim me as hers.
   I'm dressing in her clothes and she's taking my voice even –
   and then I'm wanting him. I want him. And there's no real
   logic to this love – not a real love, I know – but madness
   only. (*Slight pause.*) And yet I don't want my old life back –

'cause to lose 'the her' that is still here might lose me a possibility of a new life. It's a new life I want.

A pause.

The introduction to 'Dirty Boys' is heard.

VALENTINE. What name do you want me to call you?

A slight pause.

ELLY. Mary-Lou.

She hands him back the photograph.

VALENTINE. Do you think you could get me an introduction, Mary-Lou?

ELLY. He's very careful about who he meets.

VALENTINE. Me too.

DIRTY BOYS

(*Valentine.*) Something like Tobacco Road
Living on a lonely road
I will pull you out of there
We will go to Finchley Fair.

I will buy you a feather hat
I will steal a cricket bat
Smash some windows, make a noise
We will run with dirty boys

The light opens up and he and ELLY *are in* NEWTON*'s apartment.*

Unnoticed and the GIRL *is drawing the outline of something on the floor.*

When the sun goes down
When the sun goes down and the die is cast
When the die is cast and you have no choice
We will run with dirty boys

ELLY *goes and fixes herself and* VALENTINE *a drink.*

> We all go mad, we all want you
> Me and the boys we all go through
> You've got to learn to hold your tongue
> This ain't the moon, this is burnin' sun

ELLY *is seen changing into another one of Mary-Lou's dresses.*

VALENTINE *takes the torn-up photograph of* NEWTON *he stole from* MICHAEL *out of his pocket.*

> When the sun goes down
> When the sun goes down and the die is cast
> When the die is cast and you have no choice
> We will run with dirty boys

VALENTINE *sticks up the photograph on the apartment wall.*

NEWTON *sees him.*

NEWTON. What are you doing here?

VALENTINE. I'm a friend of Mary-Lou's. I understand that you value your privacy.

NEWTON. Then get out.

VALENTINE. But it was the oddest thing – I was walking by your building and Mary-Lou was very upset – I understand that she works for you – and just so you know –

NEWTON. Stop talking.

VALENTINE. – I'm not the sort of man that would roll back on to the streets and tell the world who lives in this apartment.

NEWTON. There is no Mary-Lou.

VALENTINE. Right absolutely – although apparently there is right now.

NEWTON (*about the torn photograph*). Did you put this up here?

VALENTINE. The photograph – yes, sir.

NEWTON. And where did you get it?

VALENTINE. Oh it's a ridiculous story!

NEWTON. I've seen you before.

VALENTINE. I don't think so.

NEWTON. With Michael – I know I have…

ELLY. This is Valentine.

NEWTON. He needs to go – get him out of here!

ELLY. So what's happening to the floor?

NEWTON. Did you hear what I said…?

ELLY. Did you do this?

NEWTON. What?

ELLY. The drawing.

NEWTON. No.

ELLY. So who did it – what is it?

NEWTON. It's going to be a rocket.

ELLY. What are you talking about?

NEWTON. We're building a rocket.

ELLY. With this girl?

VALENTINE. An actual rocket?

NEWTON. Right.

ELLY. Fuck.

VALENTINE. Didn't you do this once before? I was a boy at
    the time – but of course I remember it – everyone does.

NEWTON. Please go.

VALENTINE. You built a rocket – 'cause that's what rich guys
do, I guess – and they wouldn't let you launch it, right? This
is less expensive, definitely – but you still have this interest
in rockets?

NEWTON. Right.

VALENTINE. And why is that?

NEWTON. Because I don't belong here.

VALENTINE. You mean, the world – you don't belong in this
world, Mr Newton? Why would you say something like that?

NEWTON. Because none of this matters any more.

VALENTINE. You're building a rocket to return to your own
planet, is that it?

NEWTON. Yes, that's how it sounds. Fucking leave!

ELLY. Is the girl here now, Tommy?

NEWTON. Stop calling me that! I want you to leave – both of
you – just go!

VALENTINE. But I've come here to help you, sir.

The music to 'Killing a Little Time' begins –

NEWTON. You can help me by getting out of my apartment!
(*To* ELLY.) I'll continue paying you – just take him away
and go home, please!

ELLY. I can't go home!

NEWTON. I don't need you any more!

ELLY. You're losing your mind, Tommy! Of course you need
me – maybe there could be love even…!

NEWTON. What are you saying?

ELLY. We're staying, Tommy! We're trying to help!

KILLING A LITTLE TIME

(*Newton*.) I staggered through
This criminal rain
I'm not in love
No phony pain

Creeping through
This tidal wave
No warm embrace
Just a lovers' grave

ELLY *fixes some drinks and puts some snacks in a little bowl
– trying to normalise everything – fixing the bed, etc.*

This symphony
This rage in me

An image of NEWTON *fills the wall – it thrashes the
apartment.*

I've got a handful
Of songs to sing
To sting your soul
To fuck you over

This furious rain

I'm falling man
I'm choking man
I'm fading man
I'm the broken line

I'm falling man
I'm choking man
I'm fading man
Just killing a little time

I love the sound
Of an empty room
The screams of night
The end of love
Two beating hearts
One laboured start

One open wound
Wasted and drawn

No sympathy
This furious rain

I lay in bed
The monster fed
The body bled
I turned and said
I get some of you
All the time
All of you
Some other time
This rage in me
Get away from me

I'm falling man
I'm choking man
I'm fading man
I'm the broken line

I'm falling man
I'm choking man
I'm fading man
Just killing a little time

This symphony
Get away from me

VALENTINE *calmly finishes his drink –*

ELLY *is watching noisy cartoons on the television.*

VALENTINE *walks over to* NEWTON *for a quiet word.*

VALENTINE. There are so many things that make the world such an ugly place to live in and I've seen them – and I guess you have too. It can be truly horrible, right? And beautiful things – like friendship and being in love – can turn sour – and that sourness can turn a person blue. I've always thought there has to be something more beautiful than what we've been given down here. It's possible to rewrite this bad world and escape it. So if I can give you anything at all, Mr Newton – it will be the support and help you need towards finding a more peaceful place. I can do that – I know I can.

NEWTON. What did you do to him?

A slight pause.

VALENTINE. I'm sorry what do you mean?

NEWTON. To Michael – I saw something.

A slight pause.

VALENTINE. I think your head just imagined it, sir.

NEWTON *turns away from him and is suddenly alone with the* GIRL.

NEWTON. When do you think I can leave? – it has to be soon.

GIRL. It will be.

NEWTON. This rocket we'll build is really happening…?

GIRL. Right.

NEWTON. But what will happen next? Is there an end to it…?

GIRL. You'll be free….

NEWTON. But how will that happen? What makes you know that?

GIRL. Hope.

NEWTON. Hope?

GIRL. Right.

A slight pause.

NEWTON. Then I'm held by that hope. Only that word – there's nothing else. You're not tricking me? – you haven't sent that man to hurt me…?

GIRL. No of course not.

NEWTON. And soon I'll be in the stars…?

GIRL. I have to go…

NEWTON. I don't wanna be alone with these people…

GIRL. I'm close by.

NEWTON. Don't…!

She turns and leaves – and only the GIRL *in the light now – and a sudden jolt of unease.*

The introduction to 'Life On Mars?' is heard.

LIFE ON MARS?

(*Girl.*) It's a god-awful small affair
To the girl with the mousy hair
But her mummy is yelling 'No'
And her daddy has told her to go
But her friend is nowhere to be seen
Now she walks through her sunken dream
To the seat with the clearest view
And she's hooked to the silver screen
But the film is a saddening bore
For she's lived it ten times or more
She could spit in the eyes of fools
As they ask her to focus on

Sailors fighting in the dance hall
Oh man!
Look at those cavemen go
It's the freakiest show
Take a look at the lawman
Beating up the wrong guy
Oh man! Wonder if he'll ever know
He's in the best selling show
Is there life on Mars?

It's on Amerika's tortured brow
That Mickey Mouse has grown up a cow
Now the workers have struck for fame
'Cause Lennon's on sale again

See the mice in their million hordes
From Ibiza to the Norfolk Broads
Rule Britannia is out of bounds
To my mother, my dog, and clowns
 But the film is a saddening bore
'Cause I wrote it ten times or more
It's about to be writ again
As I ask you to focus on

Sailors fighting in the dance hall
Oh man!
Look at those cavemen go
It's the freakiest show
Take a look at the lawman
Beating up the wrong guy
Oh man! Wonder if he'll ever know
He's in the best selling show
Is there life on Mars?

Suddenly a loud burst of traffic sounds.

NEWTON *watches a light coming up on* ELLY *talking to* VALENTINE, *as the walls fill with 2nd Avenue –*

ELLY. He's not just saying-all-that-shit to make me leave? Like this is his way of saying that he's regretting employing me.

VALENTINE. Are you joking?

ELLY. It's possible.

VALENTINE. That he's making it all up?

ELLY. I mean I can understand if he was – he makes out that he's talking to an invisible girl and this stuff about another planet – like he's stepped out of the *National Enquirer*…!

VALENTINE. Can I ask you a question? You were employed by Mr Newton on the basis of what?

ELLY. What do you mean?

VALENTINE. Have you ever shown compassion for anything?

ELLY. You think he's an alien? You believe that shit?

VALENTINE. I'm not going to make a judgement! You know
how destructive that is? Having people decide that you're a
fucking lunatic – to brand you with their shit! Can't you
show a little bit of kindness, maybe?! It's pretty easy to
stamp a person into the dirt – any animal could do that – but
to allow a man his chance to find some hope where there's
none – that is real goodness!

A pause as the traffic fades up loud around them –

ELLY. Shitty 2nd Avenue. I want to be surrounded by love. I
really do.

VALENTINE. Yeah, me too.

The introduction to 'All the Young Dudes' blasts.

NEWTON *readies himself for something new.*

A light comes up on BEN *on his stag night in a bar – as the
walls fill with images of a raucous night.*

ALL THE YOUNG DUDES

(*Ben.*) Well Billy rapped all night about his suicide
How he'd kick it in the head when he was twenty-five
Don't wanna stay alive – when you're twenty-five
Wendy's stealing clothes from unlocked cars
Freedy's got spots from ripping off the stars from his face
A funky little boat race

NEWTON *turns and sees* VALENTINE *and* ELLY *drinking
in the corner –* VALENTINE *watching* BEN *closely.*

The television man is crazy saying we're juvenile
    delinquent wrecks
Oh man I don't need TV when I got T Rex
Hey brother you guessed
I'm a dude

VALENTINE *walks up to* BEN *with* ELLY. *It's immediately
clear that* BEN *doesn't want to talk to them.*

(*Ben and Teenage Girls*.) All the young dudes
Carry the news
Boogaloo dudes
Carry the news

MAEMI *enters the bar.* BEN *goes to her and embraces her.*

All the young dudes
Carry the news
Boogaloo dudes
Carry the news

VALENTINE *watches the two of them – feeling that himself
and* ELLY *are being ignored.*

(*Maemi*.) Now Lucy looks sweet though he dresses like a
    queen
He can kick like a mule it's a real mean team
But we can love
(*Ben*.) Oh we can love
(*Maemi*.) And my brother's back at home with his Beatles
    and his Stones
We never got it off on that revolution stuff
What a drag – too many snags

VALENTINE *goes to talk to* BEN *again – but* BEN *turns
away from him – as he dances with* MAEMI.

(*Ben*.) Now I've drunk a lot of wine and I'm feeling fine
Got to race some cat to bed
Is this concrete all around
Or is it in my head?
Oh brother you guessed
I'm a dude

(*Ben/Maemi/Teenage Girls*.) All the young dudes
Carry the news
Boogaloo dudes
Carry the news

BEN *and* MAEMI *are kissing each other.*

ELLY *goes to* VALENTINE *– she wants to go.*

(*Teenage Girls.*) All the young dudes
Carry the news
Boogaloo dudes
Carry the news

ELLY *is tugging at* VALENTINE*'s arm to leave – and suddenly he lashes out.*

'All the Young Dudes' cuts into loud television interference.

The television has turned itself back on.

NEWTON. Stop it! Stop it!

VALENTINE *aggressively holds* ELLY *against the wall. It looks like he's going to strangle her.*

TEENAGE GIRL 1 *appears behind* VALENTINE *holding a knife.*

The noise and lights cut – the action continuing.

'Sound and Vision' is heard playing through a wall.

TEENAGE GIRL 1 *places the knife in his hand.*

ELLY (*to* VALENTINE). Don't.

MAEMI. It's funny seeing you here.

VALENTINE *turns to her.*

Did we mention we'd be in this place?

VALENTINE. No I don't think so.

MAEMI. Just a coincidence then?

A slight pause.

VALENTINE. You were ignoring us in there – why was that? – both you and Ben were.

MAEMI. We didn't mean to.

VALENTINE. Yes, you did.

A slight pause.

MAEMI. I'm sorry.

A pause.

VALENTINE. This is my fiancée, Elly. You wanna hear the story of how we met?

MAEMI. Sure, why not.

VALENTINE. Elly loves a love story – you wanna tell it to Maemi?

ELLY. No.

A slight pause.

VALENTINE. Well it was the strangest thing. I was in a cab – and we stopped at the lights – and Elly was in a cab beside mine and we looked at one another through the windows and I knew, right at that moment that there was this big connection.

The lights went green and my cab went straight while Elly's turned the corner.

BEN *enters the light behind* VALENTINE.

For the rest of the journey I was sort of aching a little with what felt like a love lost. Oh hey, Ben! So I was going to Brooklyn – to my colleague's house – a house I never visited before. The cab pulls up outside and I pay the driver and get out and as I do – another cab pulls up to the curb. And Elly gets out. Incredible. And we look at each other with complete… gratitude. The universe conspired to bring us together.

BEN. Do you think that's funny?

VALENTINE *holds the knife behind his back – he's ready.*

VALENTINE. No. No it's not funny at all – it's a lovely story about two people finding love together but you tell it much better than I do.

BEN. I think it's best if you both leave…

VALENTINE. Why? (*Slight pause.*) Is it because me and Elly are not good enough to be around all of this happiness? Do we spoil it in some way?

BEN. Well you're spoiling it now.

A slight pause.

VALENTINE. Yeah. I guess.

VALENTINE *suddenly strikes* BEN *in the stomach hard with the knife – and 'Sound and Vision' blares.*

ELLY *backs away fast.*

When VALENTINE *draws back his hand –* BEN *slumps down on his knees.*

NEWTON *is terrified.*

VALENTINE *grabs* BEN *by the hair and drags him 'outside'.*

The music to 'Always Crashing in the Same Car' begins.

ALWAYS CRASHING IN THE SAME CAR

(*Elly.*) Every chance, every chance that I take
I take it on the road

ELLY *begins to undress out of Mary-Lou's clothes.*

Those kilometres and the red lights
I was always looking left and right
Oh, but I'm always crashing in the same car

She shreds the clothes with scissors.

She badly cleanses her face of make-up.

She mimes shooting herself through her mouth.

She then starts to dress in her old clothes.

Jasmine, I saw you peeping
As I pushed my foot down to the floor

ZACH *appears and unseen by* ELLY – *he watches her.*

> I was going round and round the hotel garage
> Must have been touching close to ninety-four
> Oh, but I'm always crashing in the same car

She's dressed as her old self.

> Yeah yeah yeah yeah

ELLY *goes to* ZACH *and they start to dance – 'Always Crashing in the Same Car' – swirling darkly.*

Their relationship still relentlessly antagonistic – they dance badly.

The music continuing as they stop and face one another.

ELLY. None of us choose the heads that we're born with.

ZACH. Sure.

A pause.

ELLY. I can't seem to point it into the direction I want it to go. I'm scared. I'm always scared.

ZACH. There's nothing I can do.

ELLY. Yeah.

A pause.

You need someone easier. Someone better.

The introduction to 'Valentine's Day' is heard.

ZACH *leaves –* ELLY *follows.*

NEWTON *sees* VALENTINE.

VALENTINE'S DAY

(*Valentine*.) Valentine told me who's to go
Feelings he treasured most of all
The teachers and the football stars
It's in his tiny face
It's in his scrawny hands

Valentine sold his soul
He's got something to say
It's Valentine's day

The rhythm of the crowd
Teddy and Judy down
Valentine sees it all
He's got something to say
It's Valentine's day

*Suddenly large black wings slowly unfurl on the wall behind
him.*

Valentine told me how he feels
If all the world were under his heels
Or stumbling through the mall
It's in his tiny face
It's in his scrawny hands
Valentine knows it all
He's got something to say
It's Valentine's day

*He slowly glides downstage like Fred Astaire – the space
around him turning black. He's holding the knife he killed*
BEN *with.*

Valentine, Valentine
Valentine, Valentine
It's in his scrawny hands
It's in his icy heart
It's happening today
Valentine, Valentine

VALENTINE *has picked up a barely inflated balloon.*

It's in his scrawny hands
It's in his icy heart
It's happening today
Valentine, Valentine

The song ends.

VALENTINE. So they have you celebrating? – seems a little
cruel – the girl's not here? She's not a living girl, you do
know that?

NEWTON. I don't care.

VALENTINE. 'Cause she's here to help you?

NEWTON. That's what she said.

VALENTINE. Something from inside of your head – spat out
and sent to save you?

NEWTON. Maybe she is – I don't know.

VALENTINE. Everything's separating – what's in the past is
cut free – and here's an apartment pinning you down and a
rocket offering you a lie – and a pretend girl stirring up what
exactly?

NEWTON. Hope.

VALENTINE. It feels like hope?

NEWTON. From all of this mess it does – there's nothing else.

VALENTINE. And not just your mind playing tricks on you –
'cause it's only right to suppose that your brain's going to
throw together something disguised as hope...

NEWTON. Then I'll take that. I need her.

A slight pause.

I've seen what you are.

A slight pause.

VALENTINE. Right. (*Slight pause.*) I wanted to help – do something kind. (*Slight pause.*) 'There'll always be a love that needs killing.' I can hear them telling me that. Always.

A light comes up on the GIRL *walking from the upstage.*

(*To the* GIRL.) Hey there! I brought you a balloon. You're a little older than I thought you'd be – the balloon seems foolish now – a present of any sort seems wrong.

A slight pause.

So do you have something to say to Mr Newton?

GIRL. Yeah.

VALENTINE. Then you should say it – don't be shy.

A slight pause.

GIRL. I was alive once. I was a real girl.

VALENTINE. And what else?

A slight pause.

GIRL. I was cut down a mile from my house and buried in the ground. And not properly dead I was lying there with my eyes closed, with no real future. I open my eyes and I'm walking down 2nd Avenue and I see you there standing at your window and I came to you that first time. (*Slight pause.*) And I'm sorry, Mr Newton, but it's not me who's going to help you get to the stars but it's you who'll help me die properly.

VALENTINE *hands* NEWTON *his knife.*

NEWTON. No.

The music to 'When I Met You' begins.

GIRL. I can't be here.

VALENTINE. She can't stay. It'll just be a moment.

NEWTON *grabs at his head like he wants to rip it off –*

A pause.

NEWTON (*facing her*). I can't do it! Maybe it's as you said and you were once alive – and now caught between worlds like me – and just an idea of a girl – but you're real to me – there's nothing else but you – you're my last hope – and how can I kill that?

GIRL. You can save me – please!

NEWTON *faces her holding the knife and sings* –

WHEN I MET YOU

> (*Newton.*) You knew just everything
> But nothing at all
> Now the luminous dark
> Feels like pain again
>
> You could feel my breath
> You opened my eyes
> For I could not see
> When I met you
> When I met you
>   (*TG1.*) Your feelings again
> (*Newton.*) I could not speak
>   (*TG1.*) You're drowning in pain
> (*Newton.*) You opened my mouth
>   (*TG1.*) You're walking in mist
> (*Newton.*) You opened my heart
>   (*TG1.*) You're living again
> (*Newton.*) My spirit rose
>   (*TG1.*) She tore you down
> (*Newton.*) The marks and stains
>   (*TG1.*) It was all the same
> (*Newton.*) Could not exist
>   (*TG1.*) You were afraid
> (*Newton.*) When I met you
>
> (*Newton and TG1.*) Now it's all the same
> It's all the same
> The sun is gone

It's all the same
But when I met you
When I met you
When I met you
When I met you

> (*TG1*.) When I met you
> You were afraid

(*Newton*.) When I met you

> (*TG1*.) She stole your heart

(*Newton*.) When I met you

> (*TG1*.) You don't understand

(*Newton*.) When I met you

> (*TG1*.) You should be ashamed

(*Newton*.) When I met you

> (*TG1*.) You should have known

(*Newton*.) I was the walking dead

> (*TG1*.) She tore you down

(*Newton*.) I was kicked in the head

> (*TG1*.) She tore you down

(*Newton*.) The edge had become
The centre of my world
The seams of my life
The streams of debris

Neither wounds of a friend
Nor the kiss of a foe
The peck of a blackened eye
An eye for the crowd

When I met you
I could not speak
I met you
Then I met you
My spirits rose

> (*TG1*.) Your feelings again

(*Newton*.) My kind of truth

> (*TG1*.) You're drowning in pain

(*Newton*.) Could not exist

> (*TG1*.) You're walking in mist

(*Newton.*) When I met you
       (*TG1.*) You're living again
(*Newton.*) Now it's all the same
       (*TG1.*) She tore you down
(*Newton.*) It's all the same
       (*TG1.*) It was all the same
(*Newton.*) The sun is gone
       (*TG1.*) You were afraid
(*Newton.*) It's all the same
(*Newton and TG1.*) But when I met you
(*Newton.*) The dream of time
       (*TG1.*) When I met you
(*Newton and TG1.*) When I met you
When I met you

(*Newton.*) When I met you
       (*TG1.*) Your feelings again
(*Newton.*) When I met you
       (*TG1.*) You're drowning in pain
(*Newton.*) I was the walking dead
       (*TG1.*) You're walking in mist
(*Newton.*) I was kicked in the head
       (*TG1.*) You're living again
(*Newton.*) It was such a crime
       (*TG1.*) She tore you down
(*Newton.*) It was such a time
       (*TG1.*) When I – when I
(*Newton.*) I was crushed inside
       (*TG1.*) When I – when I
(*Newton.*) I was torn inside
       (*TG1.*) When I

(*Newton and TG1.*) When I met you
When I met you
I was too insane
Could not trust a thing
I was off my head
I was filled with truth
It was not God's truth
Before I met you

With speed and NEWTON *pushes the knife into the* GIRL. *He holds her.*

Music, images and lights cut.

NEWTON *lets her gently down to the ground – the knife covered with her blood.*

VALENTINE *and* TEENAGE GIRL 1 *turn away and are lost in the darkness.*

Alone now – NEWTON *gets down on his knees and gathers the dead* GIRL *in his arms.*

Blood seeps out beneath her body.

NEWTON (*whispers*). No no no no no no....

Slowly he gathers himself together.

Then –

And I'm not of this world. And not yet marked by this place here. Not pinned down in this apartment – not divided into days and praying for my death – and bullied by this broken mind – and before all of this happened to me – and before the journey down here – to wake in the place I was born. And to be up there – and to feel the simple love of family. To be back there in that home – my sad past... rewritten now. (*Slight pause.*) Because my daughter wakes. (*Slight pause.*) Wake up. (*Slight pause.*) One last time, wake up, wake up. Wake up. (*Slight pause.*) And half-asleep and her arms about her brother – she talks his dream from him and keeps him in that sweet unreal place.

The GIRL *slowly opens her eyes.*

And holding now her mother and each of them the same smile – small words passed between each other as our planet turns.

A slight pause.

GIRL. And turning – and walking to you and being held – and wanting time to stop – and yet a plan was made between us, remember?

She stands – he takes her hand and stands with her.

We walk.

NEWTON. The door opens to our garden – and far in the
distance – the hill – and we walk to it.

GIRL. Countryside disappears under our feet – there's only us
two and that hill and the blue sky.

The introduction to 'Heroes' is heard.

NEWTON *tells her –*

NEWTON. This isn't happening. I'm still inside this head.

GIRL. Yes.

A slight pause.

NEWTON. And pushed further into my madness – and trying to
turn these old words into something new. (*Slight pause.*) I'm
done with this life – so a new universe I'll dream big up
there. And although always stuck inside this breaking mind –
I've stepped off this Earth and into that better place. An
imagined world. (*Slight pause.*) My new family.

GIRL. Right – your new family.

A pause.

I found out my name's Marley, Mr Newton.

A slight pause.

NEWTON. So, Marley – Do you think we can get lost in these
stars?

MARLEY. Speak some more – and we'll travel on.

HEROES

(*Newton*.) I
I will be king
And you
You will be queen
Though nothing will
Drive them away
We can beat them
Just for one day
We can be Heroes
Just for one day
(*Marley*.) And you
You can be mean
(*Newton*.) And I
I'll drink all the time
(*Newton and Marley*.) 'Cause we're free now
And that is a fact
Yes we're free now
And that is that

(*Newton*.) I
I wish you could swim
Like the dolphins
Like dolphins can swim
Though nothing
Nothing will keep us together
We can beat them
For ever and ever
Oh we can be Heroes
Just for one day

I
I will be king
And you
You will be queen
We're nothing
And nothing will help us
Maybe we're lying
Then you better not stay

But we could be safer
Just for one day

(*Newton and Marley*.) We can be Heroes
We can be Heroes
We can be Heroes
(*Newton*.) Just for one day

MARLEY *leaves*.

NEWTON *finds rest*.

Blackout.

The End.

THE NEW COLOSSUS
Emma Lazarus (1849–87)

Not like the brazen giant of Greek fame,
With conquering limbs astride from land to land;
Here at our sea-washed, sunset gates shall stand
A mighty woman with a torch, whose flame
Is the imprisoned lightning, and her name
Mother of Exiles. From her beacon-hand
Glows world-wide welcome; her mild eyes command
The air-bridged harbor that twin cities frame.

'Keep, ancient lands, your storied pomp!' cries she
With silent lips. 'Give me your tired, your poor,
Your huddled masses yearning to breathe free,
The wretched refuse of your teeming shore.
Send these, the homeless, tempest-tost to me,
I lift my lamp beside the golden door!'

ACKNOWLEDGEMENTS

'Lazarus'
Written by David Bowie. Copyright © 2015 Nipple Music/RZO Music Ltd.
All rights on behalf of Nipple Music (BMI) administered and reproduced by
permission of RZO Music, Inc. International Copyright Secured. All Rights
Reserved.

'It's No Game (Part 1)'
Written by David Bowie. Copyright © 1980 Screen Gems/EMI Music
Publishing Ltd and Tintoretto Music/RZO Music Ltd. Copyright Renewed.
All rights on behalf of Screen Gems/EMI Music Publishing Ltd administered
and reproduced by permission of Sony/ATV Music Publishing Ltd, London
W1F 9LD; All rights on behalf of Tintoretto Music (BMI) administered and
reproduced by permission of RZO Music, Inc. International Copyright Secured.
All Rights Reserved.

'This Is Not America'
Written by David Bowie, Lyle Mays and Pat Metheny. Copyright © 1985 Jones
Music America/RZO Music Ltd, OPC Music Publishing, Inc. and Donna Dijon
Music Publications. All rights on behalf of Jones Music America (ASCAP)
administered by ARZO Publishing; All rights on behalf of OPC Music
Publishing, Inc. and Donna Dijon Music Publications administered and
reproduced by permission of Sony/ATV Music Publishing Ltd, London W1F
9LD. International Copyright Secured. All Rights Reserved.

'The Man Who Sold the World'
Written by David Bowie. Copyright © 1970 EMI Music Publishing Ltd,
Tintoretto Music/RZO Music Ltd and Chrysalis Music Ltd. Copyright
Renewed. All rights on behalf of Screen Gems/EMI Music Publishing Ltd
administered and reproduced by permission of Sony/ATV Music Publishing
Ltd, London W1F 9LD; All rights on behalf of Tintoretto Music (BMI)
administered and reproduced by permission of RZO Music, Inc.; All rights on
behalf of Chrysalis Music Ltd administered by BMG Rights Management (US)
LLC, reprinted by permission of Hal Leonard LLC. International Copyright
Secured. All Rights Reserved.

'No Plan'
Written by David Bowie. Copyright © 2015 Nipple Music/RZO Music Ltd.
All rights on behalf of Nipple Music (BMI) administered and reproduced by
permission of RZO Music, Inc. International Copyright Secured. All Rights
Reserved.

'Love is Lost'
Written by David Bowie. Copyright © 2013 Nipple Music/RZO Music Ltd.
All rights on behalf of Nipple Music (BMI) administered and reproduced by
permission of RZO Music, Inc. International Copyright Secured. All Rights
Reserved.

Publishing Ltd, London W1F 9LD; All rights on behalf of Tintoretto Music
(BMI) administered and reproduced by permission of RZO Music, Inc.;
All rights on behalf of Chrysalis Music Ltd administered by BMG Rights
Management (US) LLC, reprinted by permission of Hal Leonard LLC.
International Copyright Secured. All Rights Reserved.

'Always Crashing in the Same Car'
Written by David Bowie. Copyright © 1977 Screen Gems/EMI Music
Publishing Ltd and Tintoretto Music/RZO Music Ltd. Copyright Renewed.
All rights on behalf of Screen Gems/EMI Music Publishing Ltd administered
and reproduced by permission of Sony/ATV Music Publishing Ltd, London
W1F 9LD; All rights on behalf of Tintoretto Music (BMI) administered and
reproduced by permission of RZO Music, Inc. International Copyright Secured.
All Rights Reserved.

'Valentine's Day'
Written by David Bowie. Copyright © 2013 Nipple Music/RZO Music Ltd.
All rights on behalf of Nipple Music (BMI) administered and reproduced by
permission of RZO Music, Inc. International Copyright Secured. All Rights
Reserved.

'When I Met You'
Written by David Bowie. Copyright © 2015 Nipple Music/RZO Music Ltd.
All rights on behalf of Nipple Music (BMI) administered and reproduced by
permission of RZO Music, Inc. International Copyright Secured. All Rights
Reserved.

'Heroes'
Written by David Bowie and Brian Eno. Copyright © 1977 Screen Gems/EMI
Music Publishing Ltd, Tintoretto Music/RZO Music Ltd and Universal Music
Publishing MGB Ltd. Copyright Renewed. All rights on behalf of Screen
Gems/EMI Music Publishing Ltd administered and reproduced by permission of
Sony/ATV Music Publishing Ltd, London W1F 9LD; All rights on behalf of
Tintoretto Music (BMI) administered and reproduced by permission of RZO
Music, Inc.; All rights on behalf of Universal Music Publishing MGB Ltd in the
US administered by Universal Music – Careers, reprinted by permission of Hal
Leonard LLC. International Copyright Secured. All Rights Reserved.

DAVID BOWIE

David Bowie was born in Brixton, London, on 8 January 1947. Between the late 1960s and the mid-'70s, he experimented with boundaries of musical genres and the potential of live performance and multimedia as applied to music, creating and discarding a variety of personae while releasing albums including *The Man Who Sold the World*, *Space Oddity*, *Hunky Dory*, *The Rise and Fall of Ziggy Stardust*, *Aladdin Sane*, *Diamond Dogs*, *Young Americans* (featuring 'Fame', his first US Number 1 single) and *Station to Station*.

In 1976 Bowie relocated to Berlin, enlisting Brian Eno and Tony Visconti to begin recording the albums that would become known as his 'Berlin Trilogy': *Low*, *'Heroes'* and *Lodger*. In 1980 he made his Broadway debut in *The Elephant Man* and released the Visconti co-production *Scary Monsters* (*And Super Creeps*) followed in 1983 by his biggest US commercial success to date, *Let's Dance*, co-produced with Nile Rodgers. Between the mid-'80s and early '90s, he worked with his band Tin Machine, collaborated with the dance company La La La Human Steps, and composed music for Hanif Kureishi's *The Buddha of Suburbia*.

In 1992 Bowie released one of rock's first CD-ROMs, *Jump*. In 1995, reunited once again with Eno, he produced the experimental *Outside* album, followed in 1997 by Earthling and in 1999 by *'hours…'*, the year he became a Commandeur dans L'Ordre des Arts et des Lettres.

Bowie's next project in 2002 was another recorded collaboration with Tony Visconti entitled *Heathen*. The accompanying live dates in Europe and America saw performances of *Heathen* as well as the classic *Low*, both played in their entirety. A year later the *Reality* album was launched with the world's largest interactive 'live by satellite' event and was followed by the rapturously received and critically acclaimed A Reality Tour of the world.

2006 saw Bowie return to acting with the Christopher Nolan-directed box-office topper *The Prestige*, adding to a cinematic CV including Nicolas Roeg's *The Man Who Fell to Earth*, Martin Scorsese's *The Last Temptation of Christ*, Tony Scott's *The Hunger* and Nagisa Oshima's *Merry Christmas, Mr. Lawrence*.

In May 2007, Bowie was the inaugural curator of the highly successful ten-day High Line arts and music festival in New York. That June, he was honoured at the 11th Annual Webby Awards with a Lifetime Achievement Award for pushing the boundaries between art and technology. Later in 2007, Bowie starred as himself in an acclaimed episode of *Extras*, Ricky Gervais' BBC/HBO series.

2012 saw the dedication of a plaque in Heddon Street, London (the scene of the *Ziggy Stardust* cover shoot), commemorating the fortieth anniversary of the release of *Ziggy Stardust and the Spiders from Mars* – and of course the extraordinary influence of David himself.

In 2013, it was announced that the David Bowie Archive had given unprecedented access to the prestigious Victoria and Albert Museum for 'David Bowie is…', an exhibition curated solely by the V&A in London. Marking the first time a museum has been given access to the David Bowie Archive, the exhibition has gone on to break records in the US, Berlin and France. 'David Bowie is…' has made recent stops in Australia and the Netherlands, and will continue to tour the world for the foreseeable future.

On 8 January 2013, on his sixty-sixth birthday, David Bowie suddenly and without fanfare, released a new single entitled 'Where Are We Now?', and announced the release of a new album titled *The Next Day*. Bowie's twenty-seventh studio album and first in ten years, *The Next Day*, hit Number 1 in nineteen countries, and was critically lauded the world over.

In 2014, David Bowie's fiftieth year in music was commemorated with the release of the compilation *Nothing Has Changed*, a career-spanning anthology of hits and obscurities. Bowie once again defied convention by opening the three-CD deluxe edition of *Nothing Has Changed* with the seven-minute jazz murder ballad 'Sue (or In A Season Of Crime)' featuring the Maria Schneider Orchestra. Bowie ended that same fiftieth anniversary year with the low-key reveal of the demo track ''Tis a Pity She Was a Whore', an uncompromising piece pointing toward a future of even further experimentation.

Spring 2015 brought the announcement of the off-Broadway theatre production *Lazarus*, a collaboration between Bowie and renowned playwright Enda Walsh, directed by Ivo Van Hove. Inspired by the novel *The Man Who Fell to Earth* by Walter Tevis, *Lazarus* centres on the character of Thomas Newton, famously portrayed by Bowie in the 1976 screen adaptation. Featuring new Bowie songs alongside fresh arrangements of music from his entire catalogue, *Lazarus* opened in December 2015 to rave reviews and a completely sold-out New York run – the closing date of which, 20 January 2016, was proclaimed 'David Bowie Day' by New York City Mayor Bill de Blasio.

On 25 October 2015 it was confirmed that ★ (pronounced *Blackstar*) would be the title of David Bowie's twenty-eighth album, to be released on David's sixty-ninth birthday, 8 January 2016. The album's titular ten-minute opener was released as a single on 20 November 2015, accompanied by the premiere of a short film directed by Johan Renck (which went on to win Best Art Direction at the 2016 MTV VMAs). A second single, 'Lazarus', followed on 18 December 2015, along with another Renck-directed video. ★ was released to overwhelming acclaim, garnering many of the best critical notices of Bowie's entire career. The album was his first to hit Number 1 in the US, and topped the charts in more than twenty countries. ★ closer 'I Can't Give Everything Away' was released on 6 April 2016 as a third single. An animated interpretation of the song by the album's designer Jonathan Barnbrook was unveiled the same day.

On 10 January 2016, David Bowie died peacefully, surrounded by his family after a courageous eighteen-month battle with cancer. His body of work, multi-generational influence and legacy of fearless innovation and endless reinvention will live on forever.

www.davidbowie.com

ENDA WALSH

Enda Walsh is a multi-award-winning Irish playwright. His work has been translated into over twenty languages and has been performed internationally since 1998.

His recent plays include *Arlington*, produced by Landmark Productions and Galway International Arts Festival; *Lazarus* with David Bowie at New York Theater Workshop and the King's Cross Theatre, London; *A Girl's Bedroom*, shown at the Galway International Arts Festival; a 'mischievous adaptation' of Roald Dahl's *The Twits* at the Royal Court, London; the opera *The Last Hotel* for Landmark Productions and Wide Open Opera (Edinburgh International Festival, Dublin Theatre Festival, Royal Opera House, London, St Ann's Warehouse, New York); *Ballyturk*, produced by Landmark Productions and Galway International Arts Festival (Galway, Dublin, Cork and the National Theatre, London); *Room 303*, shown at the Galway International Arts Festival; *Misterman*, produced by Landmark Productions and Galway International Arts Festival in Ireland, London and New York; and several plays for Druid Theatre Company, including *Penelope*, which has been presented in Ireland, America and London; *The New Electric Ballroom*, which played Ireland, Australia, Edinburgh, London, New York and LA; and *The Walworth Farce*, which played Ireland, Edinburgh, London and New York, as well as an American and Australian tour.

He won a Tony Award for writing the book for the musical *Once*, which played for three years on Broadway and two years in the West End, and returned to the Olympia Theatre in Dublin.

His other plays include *Delirium* (Theatre O/Barbican), which played Dublin and a British tour; *Chatroom*, which played at the National Theatre and on tour in Britain and Asia; and *The Small Things* (Paines Plough), which played London and at Galway International Arts Festival. His early plays include *Bedbound* (Dublin Theatre Festival) and *Disco Pigs* (Corcadorca).

His film work includes *Disco Pigs* (Temple Films/Renaissance) and *Hunger* (Blast/Film4).

WALTER TEVIS

Walter Tevis was born in San Francisco in 1928. At the age of
ten, his parents placed him in the Stanford Children's
Convalescent Home for a year during which time they returned
to Kentucky. Walter travelled across the country alone by train
at the age of eleven to rejoin his family and felt the shock of
entering the Appalachian culture, when he enrolled in the local
school in Lexington, Kentucky. This event informed the
character, Thomas Newton, and his feelings of shock when he
came to Earth, in his second novel *The Man Who Fell to Earth*,
published in 1963. *The New York Times* wrote of it, 'Beautiful
science fiction… [Newton] acquires a moving tragic force as
the stranger, caught and destroyed in a strange land… the story
of an extraterrestrial visitor from another planet is designed
mainly to say something about life on this one.' Norman
Spinrad wrote in his introduction, 'What Walter Tevis has done
in *The Man Who Fell to Earth*, is written an utterly realistic
novel about an alien human on Earth. Realistic in its portrait of
his strengths and failures and confusion. Realistic in its
depiction of what it's like to be an alien human. Realistic
enough to become something of a metaphor for something
inside of us all, some existential loneliness.'

Walter Tevis wrote and published five more novels: *The Hustler*,
which *The New York Times* in reviewing it wrote, 'A fine, swift,
wanton, offbeat novel', *Mockingbird*, *The Queen's Gambit*, *The
Steps of the Sun*, *The Color of Money*, and a collection of short
stories, *Far from Home*. His books have been translated into
nineteen languages. Three of his novels have been made into
motion pictures, including *The Man Who Fell to Earth*, *The
Hustler*, and its sequel, *The Color of Money*. He died in 1984.